Strong-Minded Woman

The Story of Lavinia Goodell, Wisconsin's First Female Lawyer

Mary Lahr Schier

Midwest History Press
P.O. Box 432
Northfield, MN 55057

Cover design: Kathy Kruger, Whistling Mouse Design.

Book design and typesetting: Liz Tufte, Folio Bookworks.

Cover photo credit for Rock County Court House in Janesville, Wisconsin: State Historical Society of Wisconsin, Negative #WHi (X3) 52361. Photo taken in 1892.

Cover photo credit for Lavinia Goodell photo: Berea College Archives; Berea, KY.

Publisher's Cataloging-in-Publication
(Provided by Quality Books, Inc.)

Schier, Mary Lahr.
    Strong-minded woman: the story of Lavinia Goodell, Wisconsin's first female lawyer / by Mary Lahr Schier.
    —1st ed.
    p. cm.
    Includes bibliographical references and index.
    Audience: Grades 4–8.
    LCCN 00-109380
    ISBN 0-9671787-3-8

    1. Goodell, Lavinia. 2. Woman lawyers—Wisconsin—
Biography. 3. Women lawyers—United States—Biography.
4. Women's rights—United States—History—19th century.
5. Goodall family. 6. Wisconsin—History. I. Title.

KF368.G65S35 2001   340'.092
                                      QBI00-901893

Printed in the USA on recycled paper.

For my parents

Table of Contents

THE TINY TYRANT

Her tiny screams echoed all through the two-story brick house in Utica, New York, on that first Thursday in May 1839.

The cook in the kitchen downstairs heard the sound and dropped the tablecloth she held in her arms. Coming in from milking the cow, the girl who helped clean heard it, too, and set down her pail in surprise. Maria Goodell listened to the wail and exclaimed, the baby "is calling to me."

The twelve-year-old ran up the stairs to the plainly furnished room on the second floor to see her sister, who had just been born. The baby with blue eyes and soft brown hair was about to change her family's life. Until Rhoda Lavinia Goodell was born, her parents and sister lived a regimented life of work, prayer, and reading. Her parents, William and Clarissa Goodell, and Maria studied the Bible for an hour every morning and every evening. Their beliefs forbid talk about food, clothes, or other worldly concerns, unless necessary. The family followed a nearly vegetarian diet, one based on the teachings of Dr. Sylvester Graham. He invented the graham cracker and believed that rough wheat bread prevented disease. The Goodells gave up coffee and most seasonings.

The Goodells lived in a region full of people of robust religious faith and strongly held beliefs about right and wrong. The area, which included many small towns near Rochester, New York, was so hot with religious feeling that it earned the nickname the "Burned-Over District." Many people there believed that by obeying strict rules for living—rules that governed how you ate and talked and thought—people could rise above or "transcend" their day-to-day world and live a better life. Historians call these people "transcendentalists."

From the first moments of her existence, Vinnie, as her family called the baby, was a tiny tyrant, a strong-minded young person, bent on changing rather than transcending the world around her. She squirmed and resisted baby clothes. She cried whenever she was placed in the rocking cradle her father had built for her. She would not sit silent for the long Bible studies and prayer times.

Vinnie screamed so loud and so long that one visitor to the Goodells' home remarked that the baby "should have been a boy," because she thought only boys could be so strong-willed. That is what many people thought 150 years ago.

The family had many visitors during the first few weeks after the baby was born. Some of them were men who worked with Lavinia's father to end slavery in the United States. As a young man, Mr. Goodell had joined William Lloyd Garrison and other leaders of the anti-slavery movement in their efforts to stop slavery in America. He was a friend of Frederick Douglass, a former slave who was a leader in the fight to end slavery.

Lavinia's parents were part of a group of "moral reformers" who wanted to change society in the 1800s. They felt that slavery was wrong. They wanted to abolish it. They also wanted to ban alcohol, which they believed caused poverty and crime.

Not everyone agreed with the reformers and transcendentalists like Lavinia's parents. She was born into a time of much argument and disagreement. The most important disagreement—over whether Africans could be bought and sold as slaves—led to the Civil War that divided America in 1861.

Mr. Goodell's religion and his strong feelings against slavery and alcohol often led him into public issues of the day. As a young man, he had faced a mob of people who objected to his anti-slavery speeches. He had been forced to run from the crowd and went into hiding for weeks to keep from being attacked.

Photo Credit: Berea College Archives; Berea, KY

William Goodell, Lavinia's father, worked with the leading abolitionists and reformers of his time.

By the time Lavinia was born in Utica, he was forty-seven and had devoted most of his life to reform causes. In Utica, he preached and edited a newspaper.

Lavinia's mother, Clarissa Cady Goodell, had grown up in Providence, Rhode Island. Her family owned stores and farms. On her own, Mrs. Goodell would not have been a reformer. She was shy and worked hard at home, sewing, cooking, and keeping the house neat. But she admired her husband greatly. She took his work as her own.

Mr. Goodell's work never paid well. About the time of her birth, Lavinia's father earned only $52 a year editing his newspaper. The family moved several times during Lavinia's childhood as Mr. Goodell went from job to job. He often relied on financial help from family and friends and money earned by preaching to support the family.

When Lavinia was four, friends from nearby Honeoye, New York, asked Mr. Goodell to lead a new church there. Called the Independent Reform Church, it was made up of people from Methodist and Presbyterian churches who disagreed with some practices of their old churches. Mr. Goodell happily said yes. In Honeoye, the family would have a home and a steady income. The Goodells loved the village. Honeoye meant "land of purity," and the town lived up to its name. It had ponds and fruit trees and pleasant walking places.

Since her babyhood, Lavinia had frequently suffered with coughs and sore throats. In Honeoye, these ailments grew worse. One summer, she caught a fever that made the rest of her childhood difficult. It made her skin sensitive. After the sickness, she hated wearing clothes. They itched. She ripped off any garments that made her uncomfortable.

Often her mother and sister spent up to two hours trying to bathe and dress the wriggling girl to go to church. While they tried to get her clothes on, Lavinia would escape their grasp and pull at the buttons, hooks, and strings that held together her Sunday best. Finally, Maria would hold the girl down while her mother wrestled her into petticoats and dress. Lavinia continued to struggle as they combed her brown hair.

Thinking they had finished with the little girl, her mother and sister would leave to dress themselves for church, only to find they weren't finished after all. Once, when it was time to go, they could not find her. The family searched the house and discovered Lavinia hiding in a closet, crying and whimpering, her clothes half torn off.

Her strong will and weak health led the family to give in to Lavinia in many ways. They eventually gave up on petticoats and high-buttoned dresses;

she only had to wear enough clothes to cover herself. She attended a village school, but she was sick so often she rarely finished a session. She could not run and play, like the other children, without getting tired. So she sat on the school steps during recess, watching. Walking to school one day, Lavinia met a neighbor boy named Jeff who blocked her path and told her that girls should not go to school. She tried to run around him, but he was stronger and quicker. She gave up and went home crying. When her father walked her to school, the bully disappeared.

Because going to school seemed to be a strain on Lavinia, her parents did not always require her to go. Instead, she slept late in the morning and read or played in the house on her own during the day. She loved books and stories, and Vinnie often stayed up late reading. Her family owned many books on religion, philosophy, and politics. Her sister, Maria, marveled at Lavinia's ability to concentrate and forget about her own discomfort or the sounds around her. Maria taught her a lot, too. Despite their twelve-year age difference, Lavinia insisted that she could understand Maria's work. She would quiz Maria about the older girl's lessons. Like her parents, Maria often gave in to Lavinia's pleading, and talked late into the night to the little girl.

When Lavinia was about eight, her family took

care of a cousin whose parents had died. Amanda was one year older than Lavinia, rosy with good health and a mischievous, playful manner. Amanda taught Lavinia how to have fun. Lavinia's parents allowed the girls to live "a bird's life during the summer months," recalled Maria. With Amanda, Lavinia ran freely in the farm country around their home and began to play in ways she had never played before. She sat in fruit trees, like a squirrel. They made up games in the cellar, imagining great travels as they moved between the potato bins and the apple barrels. They visited the trash heaps outside of their neighbors' homes and collected a set of broken dishes and cups. They used a hammer and nails to build a table and chairs for their tea party.

One day, the girls decided to go fishing. They owned no fishing line or pole. No matter, they said to each other. The boys who fish use a line and they spend all day sitting by the river without ever catching anything. They would try a different way. The girls carried a bucket to the stream. Kneeling on the bank, they cupped their hands under water. When a small, unsuspecting fish swam into their trap, the girls hoisted it up and into the bucket.

After a summer of outdoors play with Amanda, Lavinia glowed with health. For the first time since her birth, her parents thought she was well enough to travel a greater distance. That autumn, the family left for a visit to Mrs. Goodell's relatives in Rhode Island and Connecticut. They planned to stay several weeks at the home of Mrs. Goodell's sister, Mary Thomas. When the Goodells arrived, their cousins and aunts and uncles rushed out to greet them, except for one young girl. Little Sarah Thomas, who was about Lavinia's age, ran away from these strange people.

Lavinia broke away from her family and went in search of the little girl. She found her hiding behind a woodpile. "Did you know I was your cousin?" she asked Sarah. Timidly, the other girl came out of hiding. It was the start of a friendship that would last Lavinia's entire life.

Her family also returned to its practice of traveling to conventions and other anti-slavery meetings, where Lavinia heard long, fiery speeches. The **abolitionists** were considered radical and strange by many people of that time. They even allowed women to speak at their meetings. Lavinia listened, and thrilled at their voices. She could do that, too, she thought.

Her parents' anti-slavery activities affected many aspects of the family's day-to-day life. Anti-slavery slogans covered the cushions, the needlework, and the dishes the Goodells used. One needlework drawing showed a kneeling female slave and the words, "Am I not a woman and a sister?" The edges of the family's dinner plates were painted with the words of the Constitution, "We hold these truths to be self-evident. That all men are created free and equal."

"When I sat down to dinner every day, I read my plate until I learned it by heart," Lavinia later wrote, "learned it so well that I never forgot it. With my child's bowl of bread and milk, I drank in the question of equal rights." Her parents invited many reformers to the Goodell house. Lavinia listened to the debates and learned to argue well.

Runaway slaves also stopped at the Goodell house. Because that region of New York was known as a place where many abolitionists lived, runaway slaves sometimes stayed there after fleeing the South. Homeless people, poor travelers, and other people without money or homes also stayed at the Goodells' house. There, they received food, shelter, clothes, and a sermon.

Not everyone in the Honeoye neighborhood shared the Goodells' ideas about slavery or charity. Some tried to scare the Goodells to keep them from helping the poor and African-American runaways. One time, vandals cut a hole in their new carriage. Another time, someone ripped a brass doorknocker from the door. Hunters would shoot their guns too close to the house. When Mr.

Goodell was away, his wife and daughters heard strange noises at night. Neighbor boys teased Lavinia and made fun of her family because they helped slaves.

When Lavinia was eleven, her sister moved away and married Lewis Frost, a minister and investor. Lavinia felt the loss of Maria's company deeply. Amanda now lived with other relatives. Cousin Sarah visited only rarely. And because she did not go to school often, Lavinia had no real friends outside of her family.

Lonely and unhappy, Lavinia grew sick that

Lavinia's sister, Maria Goodell Frost and her husband Lewis Frost at about the time of their marriage in 1854.

winter. Her parents moved a cot into their room so they could watch over her at night. In the darkness, when they thought she surely would be asleep, one would creep out of bed to check on Lavinia. They always found her awake. "I don't know if she slept any that winter after Maria was married," her mother once said. Her parents worried so much about her sadness and weakness that they gave Lavinia whatever she wanted. Though it seemed a waste of money to the frugal Goodells, they bought her fancy colored paper. Lavinia sat in the parlor and shaped the papers into flowers. She planned to send a bouquet to her sister.

In time, she got used to living without Maria. Instead of long talks, she and Maria wrote letters every week. They saw each other during summer visits.

Three years later, her parents left Honeoye for New York City. Her father had a chance to edit a new anti-slavery paper and her mother believed that Lavinia must finally go to a proper school. For Lavinia, the move to New York meant new ideas and bigger opportunities.

The Long Fight to End Slavery

Slavery is when one person is owned by another and can be bought or sold, like an object. Slavery has been common in many parts of the world at many times in history. In America, slavery began in the 1600s, when owners of large cotton, sugar, and tobacco plantations brought in workers from Africa and made them slaves.

Many Americans never approved of slavery, and anti-slavery protests occurred in Pennsylvania as early as 1688. These early opponents of slavery thought slavery was unfair and un-American because it denied people their freedom. By the time Mr. Goodell was a young man, religious people began to see slavery as sinful and formed anti-slavery societies. These groups wanted to ban—or abolish—all slavery in the United States. They were called abolitionists. By 1840, more than 170,000 Americans belonged to anti-slavery societies.

However, **opposition** to ending slavery was strong in the Southern states. There, slave labor was considered necessary for the large plantations that grew the crops the South sold around the world. In the 1850s, slavery divided America deeply. There were big political fights over whether new, western states joining the union would be slave or free. When Abraham Lincoln—a man who wanted to end slavery—was elected president in 1860, the Southern states decided to secede (or pull out of) the union. This action led to the war between the North and South that we today call the Civil War.

WAR, INDEPENDENCE, AND A DREAM

It was after 5 p.m. and growing dark when Lavinia Goodell burst into her father's office on October 11, 1853. Her family had moved to Williamsburg, a suburb of New York City, a few months earlier and fourteen-year-old Lavinia loved the excitement of New York. They could not have come at a more wonderful time. The Crystal Palace had opened on Forty-second Street earlier that year. It was an amazing building made of glass and steel girders, and it housed a collection of art, modern machinery, and entertainment. But that was not all. The city boasted the famous P.T. Barnum's American Museum and more shows and lectures than a girl could ever attend. Visitors swarmed to the city to see it all.

"We are very full of company all the time who come to see the Crystal Palace," Lavinia wrote her sister. "We have to make beds on the floor and some go to the neighbors."

That day, Lavinia and a group of nine friends and relatives left home after breakfast to see the city's sights. They took a horse-drawn stage to the docks at Brooklyn across the East River from Manhattan. They walked through the navy yards there, looking at cannons and cannon balls and machinery. A man-of-war ship docked at the yards was open to the public, and they explored it as much as they could. Later, they took the ferryboat across the harbor to New York, bought oysters from a vendor for lunch, and then visited Mr. Barnum's American Museum. For a girl who had lived in the country all her life, New York was an amazing place. Her parents allowed her more freedom here and more chances to see the world.

After the long day of sightseeing, Lavinia stopped at the offices of the *Principia,* the anti-slavery newspaper her father now edited. She asked his permission to go to the Christy Minstrels show that evening. The Minstrels were a new performing group that did funny sketches and songs. Everyone in New York loved them. Though Lavinia's mother did not always approve of theater, her father consented for her to go to the show.

By the early 1850s, New York had become the center of newspaper and magazine publishing in America and an important city for anti-slavery activities. In 1852, Harriet Beecher Stowe, a white woman with ties to the anti-slavery movement, wrote *Uncle Tom's Cabin*. It told a story about the cruelty of slavery and was read by thousands of people. *Uncle Tom's Cabin* showed many Northerners how terrible slavery really was. Now, people were ready to listen to abolitionists, such as Mr. Goodell. His newspaper was one of dozens of religious newspapers published in New York at the time. His paper not only advocated an end to slavery, but it also preached the dangers of beer, wine, and liquor, and encouraged people to avoid drinking.

When her family first came to New York, Lavinia's mother began looking for a school for her daughter to attend. In the meantime, Lavinia went to work with her father. At her first job, she learned how to fold the newspapers, wrap them in paper, and then write the addresses on the wrappers. She earned 50 cents a day for writing the addresses for 500 to 1,000 newspapers. "I feel rich," she often wrote her sister. If she did not go to the office with her father, she stayed home and helped her mother with housekeeping.

She also began teaching a Sunday school class in the church the Goodells attended. It was an unusual church in that it had both black and white members. Even though abolitionists wanted to free slaves, whites and blacks rarely mixed socially at that time. One day, Lavinia saw an African-American girl crying outside of the classroom. The girl had lighter skin than many of her black classmates.

"Those other girls are slandering me," the child said. "They say I am white."

Lavinia told her that skin color made no difference and that it was naughty of the other girls to pick on her for how she looked.

Then Lavinia said, "No one can help the color of her skin. I think I am just as good as if I was black."

Soon, Lavinia's mother insisted she go to school. Lavinia already had learned a lot, from her own reading and from talking with her parents and their friends. But she lacked important skills. She spelled so poorly it embarrassed her mother to read letters Lavinia had written. In late 1854, Lavinia enrolled at the Brooklyn Heights Female Seminary, which was like a high school for girls. The Goodells chose the school because daughters of other abolitionists and reformers attended it. Although her mother worried about Lavinia traveling the five miles to school alone, Lavinia happily rode the streetcar and walked the rest of the distance. She loved being around the other girls who were so much like her. She made friends and she excelled in the classroom, studying history, French, astronomy, geography, grammar, science, algebra, and drawing. The girls visited art galleries and gave speeches. She began to write stories and often started her letters to her sister as if they were a story. Even Lavinia's spelling improved.

She loved tackling difficult subjects. In mathematics class, the teacher—whom the students called Professor Grey—decided to skip one problem in the school book. This problem, he told the girls, is too difficult. Most young men are not able to solve it, and girls would find it nearly impossible, Professor Grey said.

At that time, even educated people believed that women's brains were too small to learn some things or grasp difficult ideas like math. This bothered Lavinia, and she worked on the problem on her own. The next day, she brought the solution to Professor Grey. Surprised, he told the class that she had solved it correctly.

Lavinia's teenage years passed happily in New York. She went to school, worked with her father, and spent summers visiting her relatives outside of the city. As graduation approached, Lavinia was filled with pride and some dread. What could she do when school ended?

Although many of the girls in her class expected

to be married within a few years, Lavinia did not want marriage and family to be her only goal. She did not like housework and she did like to study and read. The summer before her last year in school, she had visited Maria, who then lived in a small country town in New York state. She saw that Maria worked hard, caring for children, sewing, cooking and cleaning, but Lavinia did not think Maria was happy being married. She knew that Maria and her husband, Lewis, often disagreed. Lavinia had been looking forward to the visit because she wanted to talk with Maria about an idea. Finally, she had her chance. As they walked in the fields near Maria's house, Lavinia told her sister that she would like to go to college. She wanted to be a lawyer. More than anything else Lavinia wanted to make people's lives better, to do good. As a lawyer, she could do that.

Despite their deep friendship, Maria found Lavinia's idea shocking. Folks made fun of women who stepped into a man's world. No proper woman would be seen in a courtroom. To try to become a lawyer would embarrass her parents and shame the family, Maria said. It was impossible and "vain" to even think about it.

Thinking about her sister's words after returning to school, Lavinia wrote to Maria, "If I were a man, it would be decided, but everything would be against a woman.

"Our folks would not hear of me going to college," she added. "I dare not mention it."

Maria again advised Lavinia to forget her idea. Stop "trying to be a man," she wrote back. Lavinia's duty was to care for her parents, her sister said. Maria's words stung. Lavinia said that if she studied law, she knew she would be "sacrificing much personal happiness. I think it is a simple desire to do good that led me to think of it."

Lavinia set the dream aside but still wondered what to do with her life. She was nearly nineteen, slender and pretty with brown curling hair. She was smart, well read, and a lively writer. Her parents had no money for college or other training, even if they would have allowed her to pursue it. She wanted to do so many things. Yet none of them seemed possible.

"In all probability, I must teach," she wrote Maria. "That is about all a woman can do, and now that profession is over-crowded with women. Our folks think of me only as a child and don't seem to think I need ever do anything."

When it came time for Lavinia's graduation in 1858, the teachers asked her to give a talk at the graduation ceremony. She was one of the school's best students. Her mother made a special dress from linen the color of cream. The summer after her graduation, Lavinia spent with her cousin Sarah at the Thomas family farm in Goshen, Connecticut. Sarah faced the same difficulties as Lavinia. She, too, wanted to get a job and move from her family's home but felt that her parents needed her. The girls enjoyed the summer together. They rode on a hay wagon and performed skits for the family. They picked berries and made jam. The next winter, Lavinia returned to New York to work with her father at the *Principia*. While she still wanted to continue her education—and had been offered financial help by one of her schoolteachers—she felt it was her duty to help her parents and to put their wishes above her own desires.

Her mother, now in her sixties, felt nervous and often was sick, or sick with worry. Lavinia took over many household tasks, like cleaning and mending clothes. She hired young women to help with heavier jobs. Her father, too, needed her. She became his chief assistant at the newspaper and called herself a junior editor. She checked the news columns for errors. She edited the news reports that came from places outside of New York. She wrote children's stories. When her father was sick—as he was several weeks a year—Lavinia edited the paper on her own.

She visited her relatives frequently and spent the

next summer with Sarah Thomas and her family. In August 1859, she was called to Canastota, New York, to visit another cousin. Her childhood friend Amanda was sick with a lung disease then called consumption. Amanda, just a year older than Lavinia, had been studying art before she got sick. When Lavinia arrived, she noticed immediately how thin and weak her cousin looked. The girl spoke with difficulty.

The next day, Amanda seemed better. Lavinia brought a book of drawings. The two friends pored over the pictures, talking all afternoon, just as they had as young girls playing in the cellar. Amanda told Lavinia how much she wanted to get better and all that she wanted to do with her life. A few days later, Lavinia and the other relatives were called to Amanda's bedside at 1 o'clock in the morning. Amanda kissed each of them. Three hours later, she died.

Amanda's death deeply affected Lavinia. As a child, Amanda had been lively, strong, and healthy. Now she was dead. Lavinia realized how quickly people could be taken from her and how quickly her own life could end. It made her more determined to do some good with her own life when the opportunity presented itself.

For the moment, though, she felt her parents had earned her care, and they needed her more than ever. In the United States Congress, representatives of northern states and southern states were arguing more and more about the rights of states and the legality of slavery. A war between the states over slavery and other issues was coming. In 1861, the war began. Many in the North, including the Goodells, thought the war between the states would be short and an easy victory for the North. Not long after the war began, Lavinia took a train trip to visit friends near Rochester, New York. She wrote back excitedly about the parades she had seen and how she had told a young soldier to "shoot a rebel" for her.

The war capped off her father's twenty-five-year crusade against slavery. She was proud of him. With several other abolitionists, Mr. Goodell met with President Abraham Lincoln on New Year's Eve 1862. They visited the president to urge him to sign a law setting slaves free. "I've never had a delegation from God before," Lincoln told the ministers. The next morning, the president signed the Emancipation Proclamation that freed slaves in the southern states.

But the war was not short. Victory was not easy. Thousands of men on both sides died. As the months of fighting grew into years, some Northerners questioned whether the war was right. Some blamed the abolitionists for the hardships of the war. In July 1863, New Yorkers rioted against an unpopular law that forced men to serve in the Union Army. The law allowed men with money to buy their way out of serving in the army by paying for a substitute. Rioters turned against the abolitionists, among others.

Lavinia and her father were at work in their office when the rioting started. The office was a long room with two desks, side-by-side. Her father's desk sat closest to the window. From the street, they heard the ringing of bells and the muffled sound of shouting. Visitors to the office brought news that rioters were attacking police, abolitionists, and freed blacks in the streets. "There was no military presence in the city," Lavinia wrote her sister, and the rioters "pretty much had their own way." The two went about their work at the office that day. The next day, they went in again and finished the editing of that week's paper.

On the third day of the riots, they stayed home, fearing that the *Principia* office might be looted. They took the nameplate off of their front door. Toward evening, Lavinia walked the few blocks to the ferry dock that led from Brooklyn to New York City. She hoped to pick up any mail for her family there. People milled about the streets. They had heard that the rioters were coming to Williamsburg that night and planned to burn the church Lavinia's family attended and a factory near their home. "Suspicious looking persons were gathering in knots and talking in low tones," Lavinia wrote her sister. Residents of Williamsburg, which was home to many German immigrants, were preparing to defend the town.

Hearing of this danger, Lavinia rushed home. She and her parents turned out the lamps at their house. They then went to the home of a friend to spend the night. "The Germans were prepared for resistance and wished the mob would come, so they could get a pop at them, " Lavinia wrote. "We were not prepared and hoped otherwise." No mob visited their house, so the next night they returned home.

The riots soon ended, but the hardships of the war continued. Clothing and other goods rose in price, as did ink, paper, and supplies needed at the newspaper. A printers' strike forced the *Principia* to stop publishing for a few weeks in 1864. The family needed more money, so Lavinia asked her sister to look around for a teaching job that Lavinia might take. But no jobs could be found, and she remained with her parents.

In the spring of 1865, the war finally ended. The Goodells' newspaper closed within a few weeks. The Goodells celebrated a victory for abolitionists, but now they had no jobs, no money, and no way to stay in their home. Mr. Goodell was sick again and Mrs. Goodell suffered a small stroke. At Lavinia's urging, her parents moved to Connecticut where they stayed with Sarah Thomas' family. Lavinia remained in New York, living with friends as she closed the family's house and business. She even sold the family's furniture.

After the war, Lavinia turned to the only occupation she felt she could take—teaching. In the fall of 1865, a businessman named Mr. Lyons hired her to live with his family and teach his three children plus several others from the neighborhood. The children, ages eight, ten, and thirteen, had been born to his first wife, who had died. Mr. Lyons had married again and had a baby with his second wife. At first, Lavinia loved this new job. The Lyons had a large, modern house, near her old neighborhood, with hot and cold running water and two servants. Lavinia had her own room and the freedom to use the family's bathroom or sewing machine as she pleased. She turned a basement room into the schoolroom, furnishing it with a large slate, maps, books, and pictures on the wall. Mr. Lyons and his wife spent many weeks at a country home with the baby, leaving Lavinia in charge of the house and the older children.

Lavinia gained a reputation as an exciting

teacher. She grew interested in gymnastic exercises and had her students stretch and bend every day. Lavinia also took gymnastic classes on her own to build her health. She taught special lessons on fun subjects, like spiders and rocks and politics. But after a few months, teaching tried her patience. The children were spoiled, she thought, and often disobeyed. She felt alone and cooped up living with a large family.

"The truth is my pupils are the children of wealthy parents and so excessively indulged and petted at home that school restraints come hard to them. I think I get considerable into their brains, notwithstanding their efforts to the contrary," she wrote. After a year of teaching and living with the family, she wrote that she so craved time alone that she considered spending her Saturdays riding the ferryboat back and forth across the river. "Sometimes they are all good," she said of her students, "and then I love to teach them, but when they get into tantrums, I am in despair."

Lavinia took refuge from the job in visiting her family, reading, and writing. While working as a teacher, she wrote a story called "A Psychological Experiment." The story shows how a young woman teaches her brother-in-law to treat his wife better. The young lady writes a letter to her brother-in-law, a minister, scolding him for not helping his wife more and not giving her the sewing machine that would make her life easier. The brother-in-law changes his ways. The letter falls into another young man's hands, and through a series of odd and humorous mishaps, the letter leads its writer to love. She sent the story to *Harper's* magazine—a leading publication of the time—and in June 1866, editors printed it.

The story clearly came from Lavinia's own life. Her sister wanted a sewing machine. The character of the minister so closely resembled Lavinia's own brother-in-law, Lewis Frost, that Mrs. Goodell wrote Lavinia that she hoped their friends would not see the story. In real life, though, it was not the minister but Lavinia who purchased a sewing machine for her sister.

The story impressed the editors at *Harper's*, who were planning to start a new magazine on fashion and social issues, called *Harper's Bazar.* They remembered Lavinia and offered her a job as a junior editor. They paid her $12 a week, four times what she earned as a teacher. At her new job, Lavinia met sophisticated, worldly people. These were not preachers or reformers. They went to theater. They dressed in the latest fashions. They did not feel bound by strict codes of behavior like those with which Lavinia grew up.

Spending time around people so different from

her childhood friends and family changed Lavinia. She tried new things and learned to get along with people who viewed life differently than she did. Though she said she was glad not to be involved in the fashion news of the magazine, she kept up with the new styles, wearing her dark hair in ringlets and a style called waterfall curls. She bought silk at $3 a yard for a new dress. She attended poetry readings and lectures on science. She even went to the theater—an activity she kept secret from her parents, who still did not approve. Her new activities led to new friendships with women and men. She was invited to dances and masquerades and was offered some chances to be married.

At one time, she befriended a doctor who knew her family. "He comes here a great deal, especially Sunday nights," she wrote her sister. "Is an M.D. Suppose I could become Mrs. M.D. if I choose. Don't choose. Don't say anything about this to anyone." She continued her writing career and wrote several articles for the *Woman's Journal,* a newspaper dedicated to improving women's position in society and helping women win the vote.

For a time, Lavinia lived in a boarding house run by a German doctor and his wife. The boarders included two female medical students and a German immigrant who Lavinia jokingly called

"The Baron." The boarding house was as comfortable a place as Lavinia had ever lived. Her room was large and warm. She had a marble-top dresser and a rocking chair in which she sat to write letters. She shared her room with one of the medical students, a "good-natured, jolly" woman. The food was plentiful and the family generous and kind.

For the first time in her life, Lavinia was in close contact with people who drank wine and beer—something Lavinia and her parents considered a terrible sin. The Goodells blamed many of society's problems on drinking. Parents who drank neglected or abused their children, they believed. Men who drank left their wives or used all the family's money for drinking. Criminals often said they robbed to get money for drinking. Banning liquor would solve these problems, the **temperance** supporters believed. Although Lavinia enjoyed living with the German family, she frequently delivered "temperance lectures" to the other boarders.

One Christmas Eve, the family planned a party in the parlor for all the boarders. The table was set with turkey and ham and potato salad. When Lavinia came into the room, someone brought her a cup of liquid with lemon slices in it. She asked what it was and the boarders all insisted it was lemonade. They had made it especially for her and it contained no alcohol, they said. Though suspicious, Lavinia felt she had to accept the cup. Her roommate, who also believed in the temperance cause, was offered a similar drink.

"In a moment, I detected wine," Lavinia wrote her sister. "I did not know how large a portion. Of course, I did not drink it. Afterward, I learned that it was all wine, only the lemon slices to deceive me. It is my private opinion that they were in hopes of getting me tipsy and so ending my temperance example."

The boarders thought their prank was a good joke, and Lavinia's roommate played along. "She drank glass after glass until she dared not drink anymore, and then she pretended to and furtively threw it away when they were not looking," Lavinia said.

"Isn't it awful? And, yet, these people are kind and benevolent and do many more unselfish acts than others who profess the sincerest principles. So are good and evil mixed up in this strange world," Lavinia said.

Lavinia's years in New York also increased her confidence in her ability to handle money. She sent statements of how much money she had to her parents. She often gave her parents and her sister money, sometimes with strict instructions on how they should spend it. By the time she was thirty, she had saved more than $1,000 from her work and investments. She was independent in every way.

In 1870, her parents moved to Janesville, Wisconsin, where her sister, Maria, and her family now lived. The Goodells had received a sum of money from Mrs. Goodell's brother that allowed them to live independently, so they chose to live near their oldest daughter and their four grand-children. In 1871, Lavinia made a trip west to Wisconsin because "we have a lot to talk about."

Before she left New York, she arranged for Sarah Thomas to take her job at *Harper's Bazar.* Sarah had wanted to work in the city for many years, and Lavinia did not want to quit her job for certain until she had visited Wisconsin. In their letters, the two women talked about Lavinia's planned return to New York after a long visit with her family. Both Sarah and her employers wanted Lavinia to come back.

But Lavinia felt a duty to help her parents and she could do that best in Wisconsin. Her sadness at leaving New York was tempered by one consolation: In the prairies of the Midwest, a few women had joined the legal profession. In Wisconsin, Lavinia might now pursue a dream she had put off long ago.

3

THE LAW STUDENT

When the train carrying Lavinia Goodell pulled into the station at Janesville, Wisconsin, in the fall of 1871, she must have felt as though she had arrived in the wilderness. There were no tall buildings like she had seen in New York. The town had no museums with art to admire, no gymnasium where she could take classes in movement, and only a few "strong-minded women" as they called themselves, who believed women should have the vote. At that time, it was against the law for women to vote.

Although it was not a metropolis, Janesville did have some attractions. Janesville had about 8,700 residents and was a prosperous farming community. Homes, churches, and businesses crowded both sides of the Rock River. Bridges connected the two parts of town. Janesville had a busy downtown with stores and shops. The many farmers in the region bought supplies in Janesville and sold their crops there.

The town had been settled about 30 years earlier. Many of the first Janesville residents came from upstate New York, as did the Goodells. The town's residents included many educated people, and Lavinia soon joined a literary society. On a hill above the downtown sat the new courthouse, with its big front staircase and a tower that could be seen from all over the city. In 1871, Janesville boasted twenty lawyers and nearly that many saloons.

At first, Lavinia devoted herself to her family. She moved into the small house her parents had rented. She helped her mother and father with all types of work, from canning food and cleaning house to assisting her father with the books and articles he was writing. Evenings, she and her parents sat in the parlor, reading or writing letters. She visited with her sister nearly every day and began to meet people in town. Lavinia especially liked a widow named Dorcas Beale, who shared her interest in banning liquor and getting women the vote. Lavinia attended sewing circles and women's clubs and taught Sunday school at the Congregational Church.

On her own, she began to read law books. She also started writing for the local newspapers and frequently contributed articles to the *Woman's Journal* and a Wisconsin newspaper that promoted temperance called the *Wisconsin Chief.*

In time, she brought her enthusiasm for reform to Janesville. Like many communities in the 1870s, Janesville was deeply divided over drinking liquor. The mayor and some members of the city council supported temperance. Other council members felt there was nothing wrong with drinking and that the saloons were good businesses to have in town since each paid a fee to the city to operate. In the summer of 1873, the conflict over drinking in Janesville grew. Three men had made applications to the city for liquor licenses in their restaurants and bars. To the surprise of temperance supporters, the council approved the first application by a **majority;** only the mayor voted against it. The council also had been told by its lawyer that unless the person applying for the license was a criminal, it had no right to refuse a license. The council decided to vote on the other two applications at its meeting the next week.

Lavinia and her friend Dorcas Beale thought the temperance people in town needed to speak out to limit the number of saloons. They felt the council members needed to know that a large number of Janesville's citizens did not want more saloons. Lavinia and Dorcas called an emergency meeting of several women they knew who supported temperance. Over tea at the Beale home that Saturday evening, the women decided to have a "mass meeting" of women in the community about the license threat. They scheduled it for Tuesday at the Janesville Opera House and asked ministers at local churches to announce it.

More than 200 women showed up for the big meeting. Lavinia, who had been reading the city's liquor laws as well as other law books, explained how the city licensed saloons and what the women could do to stop new licenses. They decided to write a petition and have as many women as possible sign it. But time was short. The council meeting was the next night. They divided the city into fifty districts and assigned women to gather signatures in each neighborhood.

The next evening, the women met at the Williams House, a hotel that was seeking a liquor license, to count signatures. Thrilled, they found that 1,250 women had signed the petition opposing any new liquor licenses in the city. Armed with their petition, the women marched down Milwaukee Street—the town's busiest street—to the room where the council met. Led by Lavinia, the parade of thirty women in long skirts and big hats attracted attention throughout the community. At the council chambers, other women were waiting. So many women poured into the room that extra chairs had to be brought in.

With help from Dorcas Beale and Lavinia, the women presented their petition to the council. One license holder, perhaps sensing he would lose business in his restaurant by serving liquor, asked to have his license revoked. The women cheered so loudly that the local newspaper said they would have been "silenced by the angry crash of the mayor's gavel," had they not been female.

One council member said he did not like to see this "unwomanly" behavior and did not like to be "intimidated and overawed by a multitude of ladies."

Eventually, the council agreed to take back the one license, but it granted several others. Lavinia left the meeting pleased that the women had delivered a strong message to the council, but she felt certain the council would have acted differently had the petition been brought by people who could vote. "If those 1,250 ladies' names had represented 1,250 ballots, I reckon those licenses would not have been granted," she said.

The temperance women, with Lavinia's help, continued their work in Janesville. Lavinia wrote about their activities for national temperance and women's newspapers. One article described in detail how the Janesville women planned and carried out their protest march. Through her writings, Lavinia instructed others to follow their example and take to the streets to stop drinking. Some historians now believe the Janesville march was one of the earliest temperance protest marches and provided a model for other anti-liquor groups. Temperance women marched for nearly fifty years before the United States banned alcohol in 1919. The ban lasted only 13 years, a period known as Prohibition.

Although reform work meant a great deal to Lavinia, she had not forgotten that she had other important things to do. She was studying law. Her mother still opposed the idea of Lavinia pursuing a career in law or even studying it. She thought it improper for any woman to enter a man's profession. Mr. Goodell and her sister, Maria, however, had changed their minds by the 1870s and sided with Lavinia. Her father believed her to be "cut out for a lawyer," and Maria knew that her sister would be bored with only household tasks and temperance work to keep her mind busy.

So, after about a year of living in Janesville, Lavinia began studying law on her own. For two years, she juggled housework, community activities, and study. "If there were a half dozen of me, I could keep them all busy," she wrote. One summer day, she made this notation in her diary: "Canned raspberries and studied law."

After about a year of reading on her own, she began to go to the courthouse to watch trials. She felt she could learn more about a lawyer's job by observing local attorneys. "It is quite an innovation for me to go into the court in this small, conservative, gossipy town and requires some moral courage," she wrote. "The community looks at me a little doubtfully, as not knowing what kind of a woman I am. But as I develop no other alarming eccentricity than a taste for legal studies, wear fashionable clothes, attend an orthodox church, have a class in the Sunday School, attend the benefit society, make cakes and preserves like other women, I am tolerated. Meanwhile, I enjoy my studies even more than I anticipated, only feel lonesome in having no one to talk them over with."

At that time, most young men who wanted to learn the law began by working in a lawyer's office. They helped with chores. They did errands. They copied papers for the lawyer. They read law books and important cases on their own. Later, the lawyer would help his students by allowing them to write legal papers or help with cases.

After a year or more of reading on her own, Lavinia, too, wanted to begin working for a lawyer in town. As a clerk in a law office, she could be "learning more in a week than I could in a month of unaided study." But none of the lawyers in town would have her.

"Just think of it," she wrote her sister, "a dozen or twenty law offices, suffering for want of students to help and keep office while the lawyers are off to court, yet they won't let me come in because I am a woman. They would sooner hire shiftless, incompetent boys that are continually bringing them grief than to take my services gratis, when they know how sturdy I am and anxious to learn."

In late 1873, she thought she had found a friend in a Janesville lawyer named Pliny Norcross. He was similar to Lavinia in many ways. Each of them was thirty-five years old. They both came from the same part of New York state.

Norcross had served in the Union Army in the Civil War and many people still called him Captain Norcross. He was energetic and fond of new ideas. He seemed as likely as anyone to support Lavinia's cause.

When Goodell came to his office to ask if she could work there, he first turned her down. They had no need of a clerk, Pliny Norcross told her. But he offered her the use of the firm's library. Lavinia began coming to the office of Jackson and Norcross frequently to use their books. A few months after Lavinia's first request to work with

Norcross and his partner, A. A. Jackson, the two lawyers hired a male student to work in the office.

She was crushed and complained in her diary, "Heaven knows why I couldn't do what was necessary." She later decided to make the best of the situation. Lavinia began visiting the student to quiz him about his work and what he was learning. "I succeed in extracting considerable information from him," she told her sister. Later, the male student quit, and Jackson and Norcross hired another young man and then another. Sometimes, however, the firm needed extra help and turned to Goodell.

She took whatever opportunities they would give her. "They seem very much afraid of me and got rid of me as soon as they could get any kind of young boy. I think they have some pangs of remorse, as they have apologized by saying that they wanted someone to do chores and go on errands for them. How gladly I would have done it for the sake of the advantages that went with it. I do not blame them, as it requires so much more strength of character than the average man possesses to do a new thing."

Despite these disappointments, Lavinia regularly visited the offices of Jackson and Norcross, sometimes working there two or three days a week. While Pliny Norcross seemed to admire her and support her studies, his partner, A. A. Jackson, never approved. In February 1874, Jackson left town for more than a week. Goodell decided to "make hay while the sun shines." She went to the lawyers' office and told Norcross that she wanted to take the bar examination in June. It was the first time she had told Norcross that she wanted to practice law, not just study it. A law student needed to be sponsored by a practicing lawyer to take the bar exam.

I want you to help me, if you will, she told the young lawyer. Norcross agreed to help her when she was ready, and Goodell went home, hopeful that Pliny Norcross would "not get scared out of it."

Goodell completed her studies and felt ready to take the test in June. Early in the month, she went downtown to see Norcross about it. He had not filed an application for her yet. Surprised, Lavinia asked why.

Other lawyers in town had told him that Judge Harmon Conger, the local judge who would conduct the examination, intended to forbid her from taking it because she was a woman. Rather than press on with her application, Norcross had decided to wait in case she wanted to "back out."

Angry, Goodell told him she would never back out. "I will become a lawyer in Wisconsin if I live a few more years," she said. "If Judge Conger refuses me, I will make him sorry for it." Goodell considered applying immediately to the judge, letting him refuse her and then raising her objections. But she feared that action would hurt her chances of being admitted in another county or city.

Instead, she urged Norcross to speak with the judge privately about whether he would allow the examination. In the meantime, Lavinia would study how other states had dealt with requests for admission from women. She also wrote to the few female lawyers who practiced at that time to ask for advice.

The next day, she cleaned house. But on the day after, she walked downtown and stopped to see Pliny Norcross again.

The judge is not sure how he should proceed, Norcross told her. He thinks he is not allowed to admit a woman. He wants to study the issue more. But he is examining some other law students in the next week and said that if you wanted to come to be examined, you could.

Lavinia said she would do that, and in a letter to her cousin Sarah that week promised to "study up in the mean time and come down on him with what thunder I can. If he refuses me, I shall try all the courts in the state and, if I cannot get admitted, shall have a bill introduced into the next Legislature and make a fuss generally until they let me in."

On June 11, Pliny filed the petition for Lavinia to be tested. She was not sure when the examination would be held because the judge was in the middle of a trial. She waited "in an agony of impatient suspense." She spent each day at Norcross' office, hoping for word of when the test would be held.

On Wednesday, June 17, she waited at the office all day. About 5 P.M., Norcross came back from court. It does not look good for today, he said. The judge has finished one trial but wants to start another one immediately. Then Norcross added that a young man from Beloit, a town about 15 miles away, was also waiting to be tested and he needed to return home that evening. You might want to go to the courthouse, just in case, Norcross told Goodell.

She hurried up the hill to the courthouse building. She had hoped she could go home and change into a good dress and collect her father so he could accompany her to the examination. He had so wanted to see it. But she did not think there would be time. Instead, she walked the few blocks briskly, wearing her second-best hat, an old dress, and dirty gloves.

In the courtroom, all of the town's lawyers were gathered. The judge walked in and sat at his bench. We'll do the bar examination now, he said, and called Lavinia and another student forward.

Judge Conger was an old friend of Lavinia's family. He had allowed her to watch cases in his courtroom and once had shared an umbrella with her during a rain storm. His wife admired Lavinia's temperance views and had marched with Lavinia to oppose the liquor licenses. But the judge did not want to violate the law by admitting her to practice, and he may have been worried about what other judges and lawyers would think of him if he admitted a woman. He told the lawyers he was not sure whether it was legal to admit Lavinia because she was a "female." What do you think, he asked? Goodell, of course, spoke in favor of her application, as did some other lawyers. Some expressed doubts about the legality of admitting her.

But no one objected strongly, so Judge Conger decided to test her. The judge called the two students forward. First three "old and able" lawyers began to ask them questions. They asked, "the aggravatingest questions that they could think of," Lavinia said, for over an hour. Then, the judge questioned the candidates, and finally, he asked the two students to write out a legal paper on their own. People later said the test was more difficult than most bar examinations, but Lavinia passed. She walked home that evening, a lawyer at last.

* * *

"I feel very much as if I had been married," Lavinia said a week after passing the bar examination. People congratulated her everywhere she went. Her father was proud of her and offered to pay her license fees, but her mother encouraged her not to set up an office. Telegrams came from friends in New York. Lawyers in town were more friendly than they had ever been. At a church social not long after her examination, Lavinia walked in to supper with John Cassoday, a prominent local attorney who represented Janesville in the state assembly. Cassoday jokingly called her his "sister-in-law."

She rented an office in the same building with Norcross and Jackson, and bought a secondhand desk. She decided not to buy a spittoon, though she had never seen a law office without one. She had cards printed with the words, "Miss Lavinia Goodell, Attorney at Law." Within a couple of weeks, she made her first dollar by filing papers for a real estate sale.

Goodell's first real case came about a month later. She was working in her office one day in July when a woman came to the door. The woman was a member of the Ladies Temperance Union in Fort Atkinson, a small town about ten miles from Janesville. She told Goodell her story. Two liquor dealers in Fort Atkinson had been selling liquor on Sundays. This was against the law, but the local district attorney, who normally would have arrested and prosecuted the dealers, was a "liquor man." He would not prosecute the case.

The temperance women wondered if the "lady lawyer" might be willing to take the case. Was she ever!

The next Monday, Goodell rode the train from Janesville to Fort Atkinson. She first interviewed the women and then talked with several people in town to gather evidence against the saloon owners. Several witnesses said they saw the men sell liquor on Sunday. With this information, Goodell went to the local sheriff and had the men arrested. She stayed overnight with one of the temperance women and the next day prosecuted the case in a local court. She won.

"The whole thing was handled so quietly, the liquor men never dreamed there was anything afoot until they were arrested," she said. Lavinia earned twenty dollars.

Later, the liquor men appealed the **verdict.** They asked that a higher court consider the case, which was allowed. A judge ordered a new trial be held in September in Jefferson, a town seven miles from Fort Atkinson. On the day of the trial, Goodell rose at 3 A.M. In the darkness, she walked with her father to the depot, where she caught a freight train going to Fort Atkinson. When she arrived, the women of the temperance union met her at the station.

They were full of apologies because Goodell had made the trip and the case had been cancelled. They did not plan to go to Jefferson that day.

There must be some mistake, Lavinia told them. The judge instructed me to come today, and the witnesses have already been **subpeonaed.** We had better go, even if the case has been cancelled, she said.

Convinced by Goodell, the women boarded the train to Jefferson. Just as the train began to pull out of the station, the liquor men and their lawyer got on board. "They looked quite taken aback when they saw us women," Goodell later said. "I was so amused I could hardly contain myself."

Goodell knew the lawyer representing the liquor men. But he would not look at her as the train pulled away from the station for the ride to Jefferson. Finally, she caught his eye, and the lawyer bowed to her.

"Good morning, Mr. Rogers. Why, this is an unexpected pleasure," she said.

In Jefferson, Goodell told the judge about the trick. The liquor men had started a rumor that the trial was cancelled in hopes that the women would not show up for it. (If they had not attended the trial, the liquor men would have automatically won.) Goodell explained that her witnesses would be late as a result of the rumor. Despite the other lawyer's protests that he did not start the rumor, the judge agreed to wait for the witnesses.

The first of the two liquor cases took nearly all day to try.

"The courthouse was full of men and women," Lavinia wrote. "I was considerably scared, but not so much so as Mr. Rogers. He was so flustered and nervous and mad that it tickled me immensely and put me at ease."

Goodell rejoiced when she won the first of the two cases, but she lost the second. She later found out that the jury had voted 9-3 to convict the liquor dealer. For a person to be found guilty of a crime, the jurors must all agree. Rather than argue all night, the jurors gave in to the three men who opposed conviction.

The liquor cases proved to Goodell that she was at last a lawyer. A good one, too.

What is temperance?

In early America, men, women, and even children drank ale and wine. Doctors treated patients with liquor for many sicknesses. Rum was one of the first products Americans traded overseas. Around 1800, some Americans began to question the amount of liquor consumed in the United States. These reformers felt that too many people drank too much and that drinking caused social problems, like poverty and neglect of children.

These people first urged Americans to be more "temperate," which means controlled and moderate, in their use of liquor. That is why their movement was called "temperance." Eventually, these reformers wanted to ban liquor completely. By 1834, more than one million Americans had signed "the pledge" not to drink liquor. Most of these signers were women, as temperance never had a large following among men or immigrant groups.

In December 1873, a few months after Lavinia Goodell's liquor protest in Janesville, Wisconsin, the Women's Christian Temperance Union was formed. This was the first large organization of women devoted to social reform, and it led the temperance cause for nearly fifty years. Liquor was banned in the United States with the passage of a Constitutional amendment in 1919, which marked the beginning of a period in history known as Prohibition. However, making liquor illegal increased crime, as criminal gangs began to buy and sell liquor. The ban on liquor was lifted thirteen years later.

THE RISING TIDE

After winning her first case, Lavinia Goodell's law practice grew. Many people came to her because they thought no other lawyer would help them. Some were women. Many were poor. The law often treated married women poorly. In some states, married women could not own property in their own name. They could not sign contracts or make decisions for themselves. Goodell's sister, Maria, had trouble in her marriage, and Goodell felt Maria's husband did not appreciate the hard work Maria did, such as cleaning, sewing, caring for children. Despite her labors, she often did not have spending money of her own. (For many years, Lavinia sent Maria money regularly, often telling Maria to "spend it on yourself.") Maria's problems strongly affected Lavinia's views on marriage laws.

When she helped women or the poor, Lavinia was doing the work she had dreamed of as a young woman, and she found it exciting and satisfying.

In one case, she helped an old woman who could not see well. The woman had been tricked by a traveling salesman into buying lightning rods she could not afford and did not need. Because of her poor eyesight, the woman could not read the paper she signed when she bought the rods. Then, she owed more money than she could pay. Lavinia helped her get her money back. Another case involved a young woman who had worked as a servant for a family. Her employers refused to pay her, even after Lavinia convinced the court to order the employers to pay her. It was up to Goodell to collect the servant's wages. Collecting money seemed strange and almost improper to Goodell, but she thought of an idea. When the family ordered a new piano, Lavinia had the sheriff take the piano as payment for the servant's wages. When the family finally paid the servant, Goodell returned the piano.

Her early success filled Lavinia with joy and a sense of accomplishment. Her sister had told her to expect prejudice and rough treatment because she was a woman working in a man's profession. Lavinia wrote, "You will be disappointed to hear of my good luck when you have set your heart on my being a martyr. But somehow I bear up under the disappointment remarkably well and I am in hopes you will, too."

Later, she wrote, "It's lots of fun to practice law, and I think I shall do as well as any of them when I get a little more experience."

Goodell's clients appreciated her skill and enthusiasm, but the male lawyers in Janesville did not know how to treat her. In the early 1800s, lawyers often traveled a "circuit" together, going from town to town, trying cases. They behaved in a casual, friendly, often joking way toward each other. By 1874, most lawyers restricted their practice to a small area, but they still liked to joke and tease each other. Goodell was a woman, and a church-going, liquor-hating one at that. Many lawyers felt uncomfortable around her. Within a few months of becoming a lawyer, Goodell learned that if a male lawyer lost a case to her, he felt very embarrassed.

It even happened with her old friend Pliny Norcross. Goodell and Norcross first tussled in a case involving a dispute over a large sack of peanuts bought by a Janesville storeowner. The storeowner claimed the peanuts had arrived at his store rotted. He refused to pay for them. The peanut company hired Goodell to get their money from the store-owner. Norcross defended the shopkeeper.

Before the trial, the two lawyers interviewed witnesses and prepared the papers that outlined the evidence in the case. After several weeks, Norcross suddenly requested a delay in the trial. Goodell believed he needed the extra time to prepare because he had expected her to make a mistake in gathering evidence so he could end the suit without a trial. "I expect it was quite a bitter disappointment to him to find that I was alright," she wrote.

The trial began on a Monday in early October. It

Photo Credit: Rock County Historical Society; Janesville, WI

Pliny Norcross

had been a cool fall with splendid colors in the trees. For two days, Norcross and Goodell questioned witnesses in court about the sack of peanuts. The two lawyers pursued the case "hot and heavy," Goodell later said. On the third day, they gave their closing arguments in the case. Goodell rose from her place in the courtroom and spoke for more than an hour, summarizing the history of the bag of peanuts and the clear obligation the storeowner had to pay for it. Her argument "proved she had studied the case with great care. She seemed perfectly at home in the courtroom," the local newspaper said.

Goodell won the case and Norcross felt angry about the loss. Other lawyers teased him about losing to a woman. While Goodell enjoyed her victory, she realized she had almost lost a friend. "I think he [Norcross] really cared more about it than I did," Goodell wrote her sister, "and got real nervous over it. You see, people laughed at him about it and told him he was going to be beaten by a woman. Norcross feels quite cut up over the result but acts upbeat and puts a brave face on it."

In time, Goodell and Norcross became friends again, but Lavinia learned a lesson from the case. After that, she often asked male lawyers to work with her on her most important cases. She wanted to get along with her fellow lawyers. She knew she lacked courtroom experience. Having another lawyer on the case helped her avoid mistakes—and hurt feelings.

Being the only woman lawyer in the state—and one of only six in the country at that time—made Goodell famous, too. Churches and women's groups asked her to give speeches. Even though she had spoken in the courtroom and in her temperance work, Lavinia had never been a lecturer. So, she wrote out all of her speeches ahead of time and then read them. She did not want to make a mistake or forget an important idea. Most of the time, she talked about temperance or about how courts and laws treated women. Sometimes, she talked about giving women the vote, which was still considered a daring, even shocking idea. After one of her speeches, a man told Goodell he would like to give *her* the vote. Lavinia often spoke with reporters after her talks and encouraged newspaper editors to write about her activities. She believed that any writing about her speeches would help her business and, more importantly to her, the causes she supported.

A month after the peanut case ended, a new client visited Goodell's office, a woman whose case would put Goodell in conflict with the highest court in Wisconsin. Mrs. Lydia Burrington was the widow of a small-town doctor—D. D. Burrington.

Mrs. Burrington was in charge of dividing up the doctor's estate—the money and property he left behind at his death. For many years, a young woman named Sara Lu Tyler had lived with the Burringtons. She had come to the family when she was fourteen, probably because her parents could not afford to care for her. For ten years, she lived with the Burringtons. Now, she claimed the doctor's family owed her money for the work she did while living with them. She sued Mrs. Burrington for payment.

Mrs. Burrington said Sara Lu had been treated like a daughter, not a servant. Sara Lu came from a poor and uneducated family. The Burringtons helped Sara Lu by taking her in and sending her to school. She had been sick many times. The doctor cared for her. When Sara Lu grew up, she taught school. She continued to live with the Burringtons and kept all of the money she earned as a teacher for herself. Mrs. Burrington said she and her husband never asked Sara Lu to do more work than they would have asked of a daughter.

Mrs. Burrington believed Sara Lu did not deserve payment for her time with the family.

Goodell took the case. She knew the Burrington case would be hard to win. The case turned on one question: Was Sara Lu Tyler treated as a daughter in the family? Mrs. Burrington said she was. Sara Lu

Tyler said she wasn't. Because there were few other witnesses, the case depended on which woman the jury believed. Goodell lost the case in a local probate court. She appealed to the next highest court, a district court, where she lost again. The twelve men on the jury said that Mrs. Burrington should pay Sara Lu $580 for her services. Goodell was convinced that Sara Lu won because she was young and pretty. Lavinia had one last chance to win the case for Mrs. Burrington. She appealed the case to the highest court in the state—the Wisconsin Supreme Court.

Goodell expected to argue before the supreme court in the fall of 1875.

The tradition in Wisconsin then was that any lawyer who was allowed to practice in a local court was allowed to practice before the supreme court. But the lawyers had to apply to the supreme court to get permission to present their cases there. Goodell applied in the summer of 1875, soon after she decided to appeal Mrs. Burrington's case. She did not expect any objection.

But Chief Justice Edward Ryan had an objection. A big one. Ryan had lived in Wisconsin since the 1840s. He was a pioneer, a top lawyer, and now the highest ranking judge in the state. People respected him. He was one of the men who had written the state's constitution—its first laws. He was smart and quick-witted, a man with a round face, smiling eyes, and gray hair. He had one big fault, though. Judge Ryan had a bad temper. Nothing made Edward Ryan more angry than "strong-minded women," a term often used to criticize women who wanted a role in society beyond the home and family. He believed that God and nature had given men and women different jobs and that they should work in separate areas, or **spheres**.

Photo Credit: State Historical Society of Wisconsin; Janesville, WI Neg# WHi (X3I) 10902

Chief Justice Edward Ryan

Women should take care of their homes and their families. Men should work in business and public arenas, like law and politics. Anyone who tried to move from one sphere to the other was wrong. It just wasn't natural, Judge Ryan thought, and no setting could be more unnatural for a woman than the courtroom.

The supreme court decided to hold a hearing about Goodell's request on December 14, 1875. Since the court had not admitted Lavinia, she could not make her own argument. Instead, she hired a well-known Madison attorney—I. C. Sloan—to make it for her. For several weeks that fall, Goodell wrote the arguments in favor of allowing women to practice.

The day before the hearing, Lavinia traveled to Madison by train. She stayed in the Park Hotel, across the street from the capitol building where the supreme court met. The next morning, she walked to the supreme court chambers. Wearing a black silk dress, thirty-six-year-old Lavinia no doubt looked like many proper women. She had prematurely gray hair and a slender build. Her eyes were large with thick eyebrows. She wore gloves and a hat, like other fine ladies. Yet, she represented everything that Ryan disliked about "strong-minded women."

"The Chief Justice is an old fogy," Goodell wrote to her sister later, "and quite opposed to me. He bristled up when he saw me, like a hen who sees a hawk, and he did not recover his vaunted serenity during my stay. It was fun to see him. I presume I was the coolest person present."

Lavinia could not speak at her hearing but sat in a spectator's chair and watched as Sloan presented her arguments. The lawyer began by saying that he would only read the argument Lavinia wrote. Goodell gave three reasons women should be allowed to practice law.

First, the law did not say women could *not* be lawyers. Wisconsin laws used the word "person" when talking about lawyers. They did not use the word "men." Goodell also pointed out that a new state law allowed women to study in any department of the University of Wisconsin, except the military department. Why allow women to study law if they cannot practice before the supreme court? Since the law did not clearly deny women the right to be lawyers, it should be allowed, she said.

Goodell's second reason for allowing women to be lawyers was fairness. The state created the courts to bring justice and fairness to citizens. Could women expect justice from a court where they could not serve on the jury? Could they expect fairness from a court where they could not have another woman speak for them? Goodell said no. It is unfair to deny women a place in the court-room, she said. It is unjust to exclude half of all people from an important area like the courts. It is also unfair, she said, to deny women a chance to earn a good living as lawyers.

Goodell's last argument was that other states already allowed women to practice law in every court. Missouri, Iowa, Michigan, Maine, and the District of Columbia had laws specifically allowing women to practice law. The U.S. Supreme Court had denied one woman—Goodell's friend, Myra Bradwell of Chicago—the right to practice law. In that case, the court denied the admission because Mrs. Bradwell was married. Married women were not allowed to sue someone or be sued, or even sign contracts. Lawyers must do all of these things. Since Goodell was not married, the objections to Mrs. Bradwell did not apply in her case, she said.

Eventually, women will be lawyers. And doctors. And business owners, Goodell said. Time and progress demanded it. The supreme court should not try to stop the rising tide, she said.

After listening to Goodell's argument, the three judges on the court adjourned without making a decision. This was their tradition. Goodell left the Wisconsin State Capitol happy. That day, she spoke with Madison newspaper editors, and one paper printed a long article about her in the next day's paper. Even if the judges denied her request, she cheerily told her sister, the case would be good advertising for her business.

Goodell celebrated a quiet Christmas with her parents, eating oyster stew at home Christmas Day, and visiting the Janesville jail to spend time with prisoners, a new interest of hers. New Year's came and went. She grew anxious for the court to give its decision. "It seems to take those old fellows a long while to digest my argument," she wrote. "Hope they are having a good time over it. Of course, it is idiotic of them to act so, but they hurt themselves more than they do me. They can't keep out the rising tide with their mops very long." If they deny her petition, she told her sister, she would go to the Wisconsin Assembly and ask for a law allowing women to practice law.

Goodell waited six more weeks for a decision. On February 16, the judges ruled that women could not practice law before the supreme court in Wisconsin. Judge Ryan wrote the decision. He rejected Goodell's argument that the use of the word "persons" implied that women could be lawyers. If the state's laws were interpreted like that, women could vote, be elected to office, and pursue all of the businesses men alone were allowed, Ryan said. This would be a "sweeping revolution of social order," he said.

Judge Ryan said he found no law allowing women to practice law. "With all respect and sympathy for this lady which all men owe to all good women, we cannot regret that," the judge said. The rest of his decision discussed the proper roles for women in society. Women should raise their families and work at home, he said. Allowing women to do other work might "tempt them from the proper duties of their sex," he said.

The courtroom, especially, is unfit for women, Ryan said. Trials often deal with subjects that are "coarse and brutal, repulsive and obscene," he said. Women's gentle natures would be destroyed if exposed to the courtroom, he said.

Finally, Judge Ryan said that if progress naturally would lead to more opportunities for women, as Goodell said, "we will take no voluntary part in bringing them about."

After the decision, Goodell's supporters rallied around her. The Janesville paper said she had "a courage that will not be crushed." Myra Bradwell, who published a legal newspaper in Chicago, wrote editorials supporting Goodell, as did other newspapers in Wisconsin and around the country. Bradwell even published a long response to the judges' decision that Goodell wrote. Lavinia also received encouragement from leaders of the women's suffrage movement, like her friend Lucy Stone, who published several articles about the Goodell case in the *Woman's Journal.*

Goodell concluded her article about the decision by saying, "If nature has built up barriers to keep woman out of the legal profession, be assured she will stay out; but if nature built no such barriers, in vain shall man build them, for they will certainly be overthrown."

The court's decision blocked Goodell's progress, but it was a barrier she planned to overthrow.

5

"I NEVER KNEW CRIMINALS COULD BE SO INTERESTING."

The year after Justice Ryan and the Wisconsin Supreme Court rejected Lavinia's request to practice before the high court was one of the most difficult years of her life. Often, she wrote in her diary that she felt "blue" or sad about her life. "Feel all used up," she wrote once after losing a case. "Feel heartsick," she wrote another day. In March she wrote, "At home all day in a state of sin and misery."

Soon after the supreme court denied her request, she met with Judge Conger in Janesville to talk about whether the ruling would prevent her from working as a lawyer in her hometown. The judge respected Lavinia, and he assured her that he would welcome her in his court. The supreme court ruling only stopped her from appearing before the high court. Lavinia continued to help clients and work as a lawyer in Janesville and the surrounding towns, as well as write for local and national magazines and give speeches on temperance and women's rights.

Near that time, Lavinia lost a case she had been working on for many months. It broke her heart. The case pitted a woman against her husband. Lavinia's client wanted a divorce and a share in the couple's wealth. She claimed her husband beat her. Lavinia believed the woman—Mrs. Leavanworth—and felt strongly that she should be allowed to divorce her husband. But at that time, divorce was granted only in extreme cases. The trial took weeks, and Lavinia presented evidence from many neighbors and friends of the husband's cruelty to his wife. The husband and other people testified that it was the wife who began the couple's many fights. In the end, the judge ruled that Lavinia had not shown "sufficient cause for granting the [divorce] decree." That night Lavinia wrote in her diary, "Finished Leavanworth case, and lost it. Too mad to say anything more." Later in the year, Lavinia sent to legislators bills for new laws on women's rights in marriage and urged the Wisconsin Assembly to pass them.

Lavinia continued to speak to women's groups and reform organizations. In June 1876, she planned a trip to Philadelphia, where she gave a speech at a national temperance convention and attended the 1876 Centennial Exposition. She traveled for several weeks in the eastern United States with her longtime friend and cousin, Sarah Thomas. The centennial fair marked the hundredth anniversary of the Declaration of Independence. Lavinia had a personal reason for visiting the fair. The documents from her supreme court case were displayed in the women's building near the fair. She also visited with other women reformers. She spent a day in Washington, D.C., and time in New York City, where she visited with Charlotte Ray, the first African-American woman to be a lawyer.

Lavinia also had a secret reason for taking her trip. She visited doctors in Boston, Massachusetts, and Hartford, Connecticut, to discuss a growth in her abdomen. The doctors confirmed that she had a tumor on one ovary. They told her to return East in the fall to have the growth removed. Her health depended on it.

Lavinia ignored their advice. She delayed because when she came home later that summer, her mother began acting strangely. Mrs. Goodell was past eighty and had not been strong or healthy for many years. Now, she forgot things, and often mistook Lavinia for her sister Maria. Mrs. Goodell flew into angry rages or babbled nonsense for hours at a time. By fall, Lavinia wrote to her sister telling her to "not expect to hear anything more from mother, ever." Between caring for her mother, her father, the house, and her career, Lavinia had no time for her own health.

She also was distracted by a new interest—criminals.

Lavinia first met the prisoners in the Rock County Jail when Judge Conger asked her to defend two young men accused of theft. She was surprised the judge requested her help. Her clients had always been respectable people, even if they were down on their luck or poor. The county paid for lawyers to defend the criminals, and Lavinia needed the money. One of the young men she was asked to defend had been accused of stealing a watch. As she walked over to the jail that first time in the pouring rain, she wondered if "he might take a fancy to *my* watch."

The criminals surprised her. They treated her respectfully. Many of them seemed so young, as if they needed a mother or father to guide them. Oftentimes, the men had committed their crimes while drunk or broke. Many of the men had no family to help them. If they had a family, one or both parents drank heavily or treated the children cruelly.

Lavinia quickly saw that the jail itself encouraged criminal behavior. The men sat around all day together in a single room, with no work or recreation to keep them busy. They had no books to read or chores to do. They spent their time talking about how to commit crimes. It was, she said, a "perfect school for vice."

She believed the men could be saved if good people would take an interest in them. She started a Sunday school in jail. She brought over books and magazines. She taught the men how to read. She helped the men start a small newspaper. She encouraged other women in town to begin visiting the jail, too. She began to take a personal interest in the prisoners and often wrote letters to them after they were released.

She described one of her first jail clients as "a real smart fellow, bright, intelligent, and witty, with many excellent qualities. He has no parents or family and I do not think it strange that he went astray, and I believed he can be reclaimed."

This man may have been a thief named Roy Cameron, whom Lavinia helped for several months in 1876. She probably was his lawyer on a petty theft case. Lavinia talked with Cameron regularly, even inviting him to her home. She arranged for a place for him to stay. Her parents did not approve of her helping the young thief, and she wrote in her diary, "Sorry to say folks don't feel as much interest in him as I do and think I am foolish."

That spring, she helped him find work. But Roy Cameron was a liar as well as a thief. While telling Lavinia he hoped to change his life, he stole from his employer. He took small things, like a child's set of tools, a suit of clothes, and some money. Eventually, he left town. "Feel depressed," she wrote in her diary two days later. "Wish I'd never tried to help him."

Lavinia kept track of Roy Cameron for the next few years, even after he left the state and ended up in prison in Massachusetts. She did not reform him, but she kept trying.

Despite her disappointment with Roy, Lavinia continued to work with prisoners. She encouraged them to study and prepare themselves for jobs. She asked many of the prisoners to write out their life stories. This helped her understand them better, she said. She helped them decide what skills they possessed. She encouraged one prisoner to become a surveyor. She helped another with his acting career by staging a reading in which he performed. She got them jobs and found families with whom they could live. She believed many prisoners needed meaningful work to stop them from tramping and stealing.

Her help was tempered with toughness, though.

One morning, a man came to her door in Janesville. When Lavinia answered, she saw a "stout, healthy, pleasant-faced boy of about twenty," she later wrote. He had blue eyes, blonde hair and red cheeks, and "the air of one who considered himself capable of supplying his wants without manual labor."

I'm traveling, he told her, going to friends. I've run out of money. Could you give me breakfast and a coat? This was a story Lavinia had heard before from other tramps.

"Give you something to eat, my friend?" she said. "Why don't you give me something to eat? And, you say you want a new coat? Well, I want a new dress. Won't you give me one? I prefer a silk, but black grenadine would do."

The tramp looked surprised. He didn't often get such a strong response when he went begging from door to door. Lavinia continued, "Now, look at me. I am a delicate, feeble woman. Haven't seen a well day for five years and have to earn everything I have, food, clothes and home, by my labor. Look at yourself—stout, healthy, hearty, strong as a young Goliath and as full of youthful vigor as

David. Tell me which one you think ought to give the other something to eat."

"I'm willing to work," he replied.

If you want breakfast, she told him, you can earn it. Behind the house is a pile of trash that needs to be buried. Here's a shovel. Dig a hole, three feet square and five feet deep, and bury the trash. Then, I'll give you some breakfast.

She went back to her desk, not expecting to hear from the young tramp again. But an hour or so later, he was back at the door. She went into the backyard to investigate and found that he had, indeed, buried the trash. On a board he found, he had chalked a poem:

> *Here lies 17 tin cans,*
> *And, 11 old shuse and boots*
> *And of my forenoon's labor,*
> *I am now a'goin to enjoy the frutes*

Impressed by his work, and his poetry, Lavinia invited the young man into the house and prepared a big breakfast for him. He told her a long story about his past—that he ran away from home at age twelve, that he liked to read, and that he tramped because he could not find good work. For two days, Lavinia let him work around her house and then arranged for a job and a room at a nearby boardinghouse. After two weeks, he ran off, stealing the watch of one of the other boarders. It seems he had told each person in the house a different story about his past—all of them lies. Goodell saw the man one other time. She was visiting a state prison in Wisconsin and he was an inmate.

The behavior of criminals often baffled Lavinia. In 1877, she told her sister about a prisoner she was helping. He had been accused of stealing books. "He delights in reading the Bible and religious books and prayers, he prays and sings hymns in a vein of the most approved orthodox piety but that does not hinder his lying and stealing," she said.

Of another she wrote, "I persecute the young man in jail by lecturing him and dosing him with tracts and sermons in between. I think my remedy will either kill or cure. You see, I have the advantage of him. He is shut up and I know just where to find him."

Goodell enjoyed her work with prisoners but thought that jails needed to be changed. She wanted them to be run "more on the principles of psychological hospitals." She wrote bills for the legislature to consider that would reform prisons. She also gave talks on her work with the prisoners and encouraged other women to take an interest in these young men. During her travels East, Lavinia visited prisons and jails to see how other communities dealt with criminals.

"I consider my criminals an interesting psychological study and think I learn as much from them as they do from me," she wrote her sister.

"One of the prisoners wrote me a letter expressing gratitude for my interest in them and saying he was going to try to live a better life," she wrote another time. "When I get such letters, I feel encouraged to work. I never should have had all this experience with criminals if I had not become a lawyer, and it has opened quite a new field of labor and thought to me."

6

"A PURE WOMAN'S VICTORY"

When the Wisconsin Assembly met in January 1877, Lavinia Goodell was ready. She had written eight bills for new laws, many of them based on her work as an attorney for poor women and criminals. One of the bills allowed women to practice law before every court in the state, including the supreme court.

Although he had no vote in the assembly, the lawmaking branch of government, Justice Ryan made clear to lawmakers that he opposed Goodell's bill. He had told them he would consider the passage of a law allowing women to practice law an attempt by the legislature to gain power over the courts. Goodell knew how strongly he felt, and so she took extra precautions. She asked Assemblyman John Cassoday, the Janesville lawyer who had once jokingly called her his sister-in-law, to introduce her bill. Cassoday represented Janesville in the state legislature. That year, he was speaker of the assembly, the highest ranking position in the assembly. Lawmakers respected him, and Goodell knew he would speak strongly for her bill. She also circulated a petition among Janesville's lawyers. The petition said that the signers supported allowing women to practice law. By this time, Lavinia had won the respect and friendship of her fellow lawyers. Every lawyer in town signed her petition.

In early February, Goodell traveled to Madison to find out how her bills were faring. She also testified before the Committee on Penal Institutions about her work with prisoners. She spoke to several members of the Judiciary Committee about her bill for women lawyers. But she left the capitol frustrated.

"Spent a stupid afternoon in Cassoday's room waiting for men to come to me," she wrote in her diary that night, "and finally had them brought to me. Talked with several of the Judiciary Committee."

The lawmakers surprised Goodell when they told her why many legislators did not want to pass the bill for women lawyers. They had no objections to her or women lawyers, but they feared that passing the law might harm Judge Ryan's health. The chief justice's disapproval of women seeking careers was strongly felt and widely known. The chief justice had been seriously ill most of that winter. The lawmakers worried that if he heard the bill had passed, the shock might kill him.

The bill finally did pass. On March 12, Goodell wrote in her diary, "A snowy day. Took lunch at office. Fried eggs and toast. Called on Cassoday who told me my Supreme Court bill passed, at which I greatly rejoiced."

She later wrote her sister about her visit to the assembly. She added that her bill had passed, and "the Chief Justice still lives."

Despite the new law and her reputation as a skilled lawyer, Goodell's legal business suffered in 1877 and 1878. She was frequently sick. The growth in her abdomen had not been removed, and she was in pain often. Her parents also required more help, and for several months in 1877, Sarah Thomas moved to Janesville to live with the family. Sarah's understanding, friendship, and good humor sustained Lavinia during those difficult months. Lavinia also had two other new friends. Kate Kane and Angie King both were studying law in Janesville. King had been studying for many years at home on her own but had never taken the bar examination. Kane worked in Pliny Norcross' office and planned to take the bar examination as soon as she was ready. Both women frequently visited Goodell's home and office, and gave her the chance to talk about law among friends.

Throughout 1877, the behavior of Lavinia's mother grew more and more strange, so that even with Sarah's help, Lavinia and her father could not care for her. In July 1877, Lavinia and her father sadly placed Mrs. Goodell in a mental hospital. Lavinia moved her office home that summer to be closer to her father, who was lonely. Then, on February 14, 1878, Goodell's father died. William Goodell was eighty-five. In his later years, Mr. Goodell had been her biggest supporter. She missed him terribly. In her sadness, Goodell threw herself into writing the story of his life in a memorial pamphlet.

With her mother's care assured, Lavinia finally decided to have the operation that doctors had told her to have two years earlier. In April 1878, she traveled to New York City for the dangerous surgery. She knew she might not live through it. She spent weeks in bed and at one time weighed as little as eighty-eight pounds. While she was in New York, her mother died. Doctors and nurses hid the news from her for several days, fearing that it would keep her from getting well.

Slowly, she gained back her strength. Through

the long recovery, she often wrote how much she wanted to get back to work. Even during her recovery, she could not stop working. She attended the Woman's Congress in Providence, Rhode Island, a few months after her operation and gave two speeches supporting the vote for women.

Finally, in late 1878, she returned to Janesville. She rented rooms in a house and a small office in downtown Janesville. She began taking cases and settling the estate left by her father and mother. She also renewed friendships in the town, including with Kate Kane and Angie King.

On January 10, 1879, Goodell walked over to the courthouse on an important matter. She had no case there that day, but she wanted to see something. In the courtroom, Angie King was taking her bar examination. King had grown up in Janesville and had been studying law for years. She had decided at last to take the bar exam. Kate Kane had been admitted in 1878 while Lavinia was away, the second female lawyer in the state.

Goodell took a seat in the courtroom, ready to watch her friend undergo the same test she had taken nearly five years earlier. The examination was "severe and protracted," Goodell noted. Young men studying law now understood that if they were examined with a woman student they could expect a tough time, she told her sister.

But King passed and Lavinia congratulated her. The day after the examination, King formed a law partnership with Goodell. It was the first all-female law firm in the state. Elizabeth Cady Stanton, the noted leader of the women's **suffrage movement**, knew of Lavinia from her frequent articles about women's rights and law. To mark the formation of the new firm, Stanton sent King and Goodell drawings of herself and Susan B. Anthony, her fellow suffragist, to hang in their offices.

That spring, the firm of Goodell and King took on a new and interesting criminal case. The case involved Tom Ingalls, whom Lavinia had met through her work at the jail. Tom had a long history of trouble with the law. He had been sent to prison three years earlier for stealing a man's coat. In October 1878, he was accused of stealing clothes from a tailor shop.

The crime had been committed with unusual care. The owner of the Janesville shop had carefully locked the door and window that night. The burglar used a straight-edged razor to cut a hole in the glass of the window. He cut the hole just large enough for a man to stick his hand and arm through the hole. Then, the burglar removed a nail that held the window sash in place. With the nail gone, the window could be opened. The burglar removed his arm and opened the window. About one hundred dollars worth of men's clothing was taken from the store that night.

Tom Ingalls claimed he did not do it, but he knew about the theft. He said a friend of his, named Jacob Bender, committed the crime. Bender told Ingalls about it and shared some of the loot. Police discovered the clothes with Bender, but Bender said it was Ingalls who had given him the clothing after committing the crime.

Tom Ingalls told Goodell he had spent the evening of the burglary drinking with friends. Tom's friends confirmed that he had been drunk all night long. Lavinia believed him and used his drunkenness to defend him against the charge. She argued that a drunken person would not have the steadiness of hand needed to carry out such a precise job.

It was an unusual defense. Usually lawyers used drunkenness as a defense only to claim that a person did not know what he was doing. Tom Ingalls did not claim that. He knew where he was and what he was doing. Goodell claimed only that he was physically incapable of committing the crime because he would have been too drunk to cut glass so precisely.

The case came to trial in May and took several days to complete. Kate Kane, Angie King, and Lavinia Goodell had prepared the case together, but Lavinia argued it in court. Goodell called Albert Jones, a friend of Ingalls', to testify. When questioned by Goodell, Jones said he had been with Ingalls on the night of the crime.

"Where and in what condition was he?" Goodell asked.

The prosecuting attorney objected to the question. Ingalls' condition did not matter, he said. Ingalls already had testified he was not so drunk that he had no memory of the night. Goodell's longtime friend, Judge Harmon Conger, presided over the trial.

"I don't see the propriety of taking up the time to show his condition," the judge told Goodell. "The only question is whether he was so under the influence of liquor that he did not know what he was doing."

She replied, "We desire to show that he was in such a condition that he could not have done this job as neatly as it was done."

"I don't understand that you are entitled to show that," the judge said.

Goodell argued back. "We offer the evidence for the purpose of showing that the defendant was physically and mentally incapable of committing the burglary as it was shown to have been done," she said.

Judge Conger ruled against her and forbid

Goodell from asking any questions about Ingalls' condition. The trial lasted the rest of the day. When Conger gave his instructions to the jury, he said again that they could not consider whether Tom Ingalls was physically able to have carried out the crime.

The jury deliberated only five minutes before returning a verdict of guilty.

"I am so sorry," Goodell wrote in her diary that night. "I think him innocent and now more than ever. The evidence was so thin."

Ten days later, she heard that Jacob Bender was "breathing out threatenings and slander against me, and [I am] half resolved to invest in a pistol but went to a prayer meeting instead."

She also appealed Tom's case to the Wisconsin Supreme Court.

A few weeks before the trial, Goodell had applied for the second time for the right to practice before the state supreme court. She had Wisconsin law on her side this time, but Justice Ryan was still alive and felt as strongly as ever against her. With only three judges on the high court, she knew she would have to convince both of the other two of her right to practice law.

Goodell took no chances. She prepared a long argument that made reference to all of the states allowing women full rights before the bar. She also asked I. C. Sloan, who had presented her arguments a few years earlier, to make the presentation again.

"It is thought that Judge Ryan will fight to the last," she wrote her sister.

The supreme court listened to the arguments on April 21 but did not make a decision until June. On June 18, Goodell was admitted to practice before the state supreme court. The court's vote was 2-1, with Justice Ryan objecting.

That summer and fall, Goodell worked on the brief she would present to the supreme court on Tom's behalf. Her life was changing again.

In the summer of 1879, Goodell and Angie King had a dispute over money that disturbed Goodell greatly. Her diary contains several notes about "trouble about partnership accounts" and "another horrid financial struggle." They ended their business but remained friends.

With her parents dead and her partnership with Angie King broken, Goodell saw no reason to remain in Janesville. Her sister, Maria, lived in Michigan, but Goodell did not want to move there. She considered moving to Milwaukee, where Kate Kane had begun to practice law but decided she would enjoy life more in Madison, the state capital. She continued her work with temperance and women's rights causes and felt it was best to be close to the seat of government. Madison also offered good libraries and some close friends.

That fall, the forty-year-old Goodell moved to Madison, where she rented an office with another lawyer. She immediately went to the local jail to continue her work with prisoners. The friendship of criminals was a bright spot in a dark time for Goodell.

"The kindness of the boys comforted me," she wrote. "No one else has been so cordial and kind since I came to Madison."

Goodell's illness, which was cancer, had returned. At times, she could barely lift a wash basin. Other times she was as strong, lively, and outspoken as ever. Friends urged her to give up practicing law and concentrate on writing, but she refused.

"I shall practice law as long as I can hold together," she told her sister.

In early 1880, her illness took her to Milwaukee. She first visited a spa where she hoped to get relief from her pain. Later, she moved to the home of a former neighbor, where a nurse cared for her. It was there on March 11, 1880, that she heard word on the high court's ruling in Tom's case.

The court had considered her argument and overturned Judge Conger's decision. Tom would be released from prison and given a new trial. Goodell had won her case.

"It was," she wrote her sister, "a pure woman's victory."

Epilogue

"THERE IS SO MUCH I WANT TO BE DOING."

Lavinia Goodell died March 31, 1880, three weeks after hearing the news of her supreme court victory. She was forty years old.

She died with her sister, Maria, and her cousin, Sarah, nearby, as they had been for much of her life. At the time of her death, Lavinia thought she had fallen short of many of her goals.

"There is so much I want to be doing," she wrote her sister that March, "articles to write, lawsuits to run, investments to make, and the world to straighten out generally."

It would take forty more years before many of Lavinia's causes gained popular support. In 1919, the country did ban alcohol—although the experiment lasted only until 1933. In 1920, women did at last earn the right to vote. Some of Lavinia Goodell's ideas for reforming the treatment of prisoners were instituted but not for decades after her death.

Lavinia's death was felt deeply by those around her. The women's rights movement in Wisconsin stumbled in the 1880s, in part because it had lost her leadership. Lavinia alone among the women reformers had the ability to bring women's concerns to the press, the legislature, and the courts. Prisoners and criminals missed her, too. When her sister went through Lavinia's papers after her death, she found hundreds of letters from prisoners. Many of the letters began, "Dear Mother."

Lavinia Goodell accomplished more than she knew. She was, at the time of her death, perhaps the best-known female lawyer in the country. Justice Ryan and his strong objections to her had made her famous. The conflict between them raised the issue of whether women could be lawyers—an idea people had hardly even considered before. She was respected and admired by lawyers, judges, lawmakers, reporters, and criminals alike. They found her to be smart and honest. She spoke her mind and treated others kindly. She could laugh at herself and she used humor to face difficulties. She reached out to help those who needed it most: the poor, women, and people in trouble.

Her fight to practice law before the Wisconsin Supreme Court opened the legal profession to women in Wisconsin. The case also served as a reminder to other states that women could not be kept out of the profession forever. Today, more than one-quarter of all lawyers are women, and half of all law school students are women.

Lavinia Goodell would be pleased.

Glossary

abolitionist — A person who wishes to abolish, or end, slavery

majority — The larger number or part of something, usually more than half, such as "the majority of voters"

opposition — The act of opposing, or taking a position against, an idea, person, or behavior

Prohibition — A law, order, or decree that forbids something. Also the period from 1920 to 1933, during which alcoholic beverages were illegal in the United States

spheres — The areas of life in which a person acts and has influence

suffrage movement — An organized effort to gain the right to vote for women

subpeona — A legal paper requiring a person to appear in court and answer questions about an event or issue

temperance — Being moderate or controlled. Also to avoid drinking alcoholic beverages

verdict — A decision reached by a jury at the end of a trial

Note on Sources

How do we know that Lavinia Goodell was a cranky baby? Or that she missed school often? Or that she called the chief justice of the Wisconsin Supreme Court "an old fogy"?

Without telephones or the Internet, people of Goodell's time communicated most often in writing. Many people also kept diaries, daily records of what they did and how they felt. The Goodell family was no different. When they did not live in the same town, members of the Goodell family wrote to each other at least once a week. They also wrote articles and sermons, and William Goodell, Lavinia's father, wrote several books.

After Lavinia's death, her sister, Maria Goodell Frost, saved Lavinia's letters, diaries, and other writings. Maria's son, William Goodell Frost, saved them after his mother died in 1899. William Frost served many years as president of Berea College in Berea, Kentucky. Because the Goodells were so involved in important issues of the time, William Frost gave the college all of his family's papers, letters, articles, and speeches for safekeeping. Those papers remain today in the archives of Berea College, where historians and writers can read them and learn about the Goodell family. The records include a 243-page, handwritten biography of Lavinia Goodell that Maria wrote. (This is where most of the information about Lavinia's childhood comes from.) They also include several years of Lavinia's diaries and hundreds of letters between Lavinia and Maria, Lavinia's parents and Maria, and between Lavinia and her friend Sarah Thomas. Lavinia Goodell also wrote many articles during her life for women's newspapers that record what she thought about her work as a lawyer and reformer.

These sources, which are called primary sources because they are the first records of history, were used extensively in researching and writing this story of Lavinia Goodell's life. However, they were not the only sources of information for this book. Newspaper records, pictures, and court records kept at the State Historical Society of Wisconsin in Madison, Wisconsin, and the Rock County Historical Society in Janesville, Wisconsin, also contributed information about Lavinia Goodell, Chief Justice Edward Ryan, and other Janesville residents such as Pliny Norcross and Judge Harmon Conger. An article on Lavinia Goodell appeared in the *Wisconsin Magazine of History* in

1991. The author of that article, Catherine B. Cleary, was the first to unearth much of the information about Lavinia's life and career.

Other books about Wisconsin history, women lawyers, and the nineteenth century were consulted for information about the world that Lavinia Goodell lived in. Historians call these types of records secondary sources. Here are a few of the books used for important background information in writing this book.

America's First Woman Lawyer: The Biography of Myra Bradwell, by Jane M. Friedman, Prometheus Books, Buffalo, N.Y., 1993.

Barred from the Bar: A History of Women in the Legal Profession, by Hedda Garza, Franklin Watts Publishing, Danbury, Conn., 1996.

The Burned-over District: The Social and Intellectual History of Enthusiastic Religion in Western New York, 1800–1850, by Whitney R. Cross, Cornell University Press, Ithaca, N.Y., 1950.

The Other Civil War: American Women in the Nineteenth Century, by Catherine Clinton, Hill & Wang, New York, N.Y., 1984.

On Wisconsin Women: Working for Their Rights from Settlement to Suffrage, by Genevieve G. McBride, University of Wisconsin Press, Madison, Wis., 1993.

Acknowledgements

This book would not have been written without the help and encouragement of many people. Research was conducted at the libraries of the State Historical Society of Wisconsin in Madison, Wisconsin; the Rock County Historical Society in Janesville, Wisconsin; the Archives of Berea College in Berea, Kentucky; and Carleton College in my hometown of Northfield, Minnesota. All the librarians and archivists I encountered were knowledgeable, helpful, and supportive. Special thanks go to Gerald Roberts, Shannon Wilson, and Sidney Farr at Berea College; Maurice J. Montgomery of the Rock County Historical Society; and Harold Miller, who unearthed information about Lavinia Goodell's prison boys from records of the State Historical Society of Wisconsin.

Excellent help in editing the manuscript came from Marybeth Lorbiecki and Paula Schanilec. Victoria Straughn provided helpful comments and insight. Thanks also go to Connie Sansome for her advice and guidance on publishing and to Liz Tufte and Kathy Kruger for a beautiful book design. Finally, I would like to thank my husband, Steve Schier, for his unfailing support for this book and my writing, and especially my longtime friend Julie Jensen, who gave me the idea and was always ready with advice and encouragement.

Index

Mary Lahr Schier is a freelance journalist with an interest in women's history. She lives in Northfield, Minnesota, with her husband and their two strong-minded daughters.